MW01233366

THE MUNSINGER CLEMENS GARDENS

THE MUNSINGER CLEMENS GARDENS

The Jewel
of St. Cloud

STEPHEN R. FULLER

Copyright © 2014 Stephen R. Fuller.
All rights reserved.
ISBN: 978-0-692-34491-0
All photos by the author, unless otherwise noted.
Printed in the United States of America by
Sentinel Printing, St. Cloud, MN
Prepress work by
Appletree Book Services, St. Cloud, MN
www.appletreebookservices.com

Contents

Munsinger Roads 2014 Munsinger Photo Contest Winner. Photo courtesy of John M. Scott.

Clemens Yellow Garden.

Foreword

IN THE TRAVEL SECTION OF THE SEPTEMBER 16, 2012, Minneapolis *Star-Tribune*, an article entitled "Weekend Away to St. Cloud, Minnesota" recommends "If you only have a few hours, beeline for the Clemens and Munsinger Gardens, two of Minnesota's best (and most colorful) attractions."

The Munsinger Clemens Gardens are special and unique to the St. Cloud community. A tremendous source of community pride, these gardens not only are viewed by thousands of residents and visitors every year but are also incorporated into the fabric of the community. Weddings, family reunions, concerts, plays, art fairs and other special events are now held there.

Their special beauty and unique design reflect a wonderful sense of creative talent that exists in the St. Cloud community. Beginning with Joseph Munsinger, who possessed no formal training but had a tremendous eye for floral beauty, the Gardens throughout their long and varied history have grown and developed into one of the finest public gardens in the United States.

As a resident of St. Cloud for forty years and an ardent admirer of the Munsinger Clemens Gardens, I was dismayed to walk into the Clemens Gardens gift shop in the summer of 2012 and learn that no one had put together a book on the Gardens. Hence this undertaking.

As more people have found out about this project, they have cheered me on and been very supportive. Special thanks go to local historian Bill Morgan and to Kenton Frohrip for their encouragement and advice, to the Stearns County Historical Society staff, especially to both John Decker and Sarah Warnke in the research division, to the *St. Cloud Daily Times*, and for the willingness of Scott Zlotnik, David Morreim and Nia Primus to share their knowledge and expertise regarding the history and maintenance of the gardens. The artistic representations of the Munsinger Clemens Gardens appear in this book with the kind permission of Beleo and Kathleen Petheo, Jack Kelly, R.C. McCoy, and Mike Pokilek. For that I am grateful. Special mention must also go to Ozzie Mayers, Timothy Fuller, and

Donna Gorrell for reviewing the copy of this book and to Ann Marie Johnson who wrote on both gardens for her Master's thesis at St. Cloud State University (completed in 1998). Ann Marie did a very thorough history of St. Cloud, its parks, and the beginnings of the Munsinger Clemens Gardens. Ann Marie has been most gracious in allowing my "lifting" of information from her thesis. I am also indebted to the numerous excellent articles on the various Clemens Gardens written by Carole Pike, Idella Moberg, Joan Andersen and others for the Munsinger Clemens Botanical Society newsletter. Mary Sue Potter, daughter of Bill Clemens, has provided updates, photos and corrections on the Clemens legacy which have been very much appreciated. Special thanks goes to Seal Dwyer for her editing of this book and for encouraging me to expand the historical section. Thanks also goes to Brandon Paumen for his formatting the contents of this book.

The photos in this book reflect the Gardens throughout the regular season, including tulips in the spring, flowers in their various stages from early to late summer, and some fall shots. Except where indicated, all photos are my own.

It is hoped that a book like this one not only will provide a keepsake for those who come to view the Gardens and become enthralled with them, as so many of us have, but will also provide a permanent legacy of the history and the rich development of the Munsinger Clemens Gardens.

It is to all the people of St. Cloud, Minnesota, who share my enthusiasm for this precious and enduring resource, that I dedicate this book.

Stephen Fuller
St. Cloud, Minnesota 2015

Fountain in the Perennial Garden.

Introduction

THE MUNSINGER CLEMENS GARDENS IN SOUTHEAST St. Cloud, Minnesota, are considered a "gem among Minnesota public gardens." Spanning twenty-one acres, these Gardens are enjoyed by over 300,000 visitors each year. They are among the finest public flower gardens in the United States. They have become a major public landmark and have made manifold contributions of permanent cultural value to the city. They provide public open spaces in which visitors can relax and become refreshed in an atmosphere of considerable beauty. For local residents, these gardens have become a gathering place for numerous special events.

The Gardens' season runs from the end of May until around Halloween. Before and after the season, twenty-five paid workers and a varying number of volunteers are involved in planting of the flowers and maintenance of the Gardens. Over 1800 roses are displayed in the Rose Garden area alone.

Munsinger Clemens Gardens are a blend of European and American design, mirroring a trend of public garden development throughout the United States. From the beginning, American garden design drew its inspiration from Europe, especially England. The flower garden that Thomas Jefferson established at his Monticello residence in Virginia was based on the English landscape garden style, which includes winding paths and large expanses of green. George Washington and Jefferson are considered two of our nation's first gardeners.

The establishment of public gardens and parks in America began during the nineteenth century. These developments were the result of efforts by concerned citizens in various regions. America's first landscape gardener, Andrew Jackson Donning, advocated an English landscape style that emphasized taking advan-

Opposite top: Planting.
Opposite bottom, left: Weeding.
Opposite bottom, right: Planting the urns.

Edging.

tage of the natural beauty of each site.

The public parks movement got its official start in 1852 with the creation of Central Park in New York City. Frederick Law Olmsted, the designer of Central Park, felt that gardening was the most decorative of all art forms. Olmsted went on to design public parks in Brooklyn (1866), Boston (1880), and the landscape for the World's Columbian Exposition in Chicago (1893).

The first public botanical garden was established in St. Louis, Missouri (1859), by Henry Shaw. The Missouri Botanical Garden, though featuring the first Japanese garden built in America, was inspired by the gardens of Chatsworth in Devonshire, England.

Weeding.

Botanical gardens became more numerous, including in Minnesota in the late nineteenth century. By the early twentieth century, public gardens in Minnesota had become integral to community life. In 1907, the Eloise Butler Wildflower Garden and Bird Sanctuary was established by a botany teacher from Maine on twenty-two acres of land in Minneapolis. This garden is the oldest public wildflower garden in the United States. Minnesota also created the second oldest public rose garden in the country. The Lyndale Park Rose Garden, developed by Theodore Wirth, is located near Lake Harriet in Minneapolis.

Smaller towns such as St. Cloud began to follow suit, and public gardens became important in the development of the city of St. Cloud.

The Wishing Well Bridge.

A bed of hostas in the shade of pine trees.

Torenia have replaced *impatiens wallerenia*.

Hostas and coleus provide texture in the shade of the giant pines.

1970 Photo of Munsinger Garden. Photo Courtesy Stearns History Museum.

How It All Began

ORIGINALLY ST. CLOUD CONSISTED OF 320 ACRES, bordered by the Mississippi River on the east, by ravines on both the north and south, and by Lake George near its western border. The town began as three independent settlements. "Middle Town" was founded in 1853 when John Lynn Wilson purchased 320 acres from Ole Bergeson, a "Norwegian squatter," for $100. Populated mainly by German Catholics, "Middle Town" was situated between two rivers that originally connected Lake George to the Mississippi.

"Upper Town," which was originally called "Acadia," was founded by General Sylvanus B. Lowry of Tennessee and was populated by wealthy slave-owning Southerners. "Lower Town," populated by "Yankee merchants," was established by George Fuller Brott of New York. John L. Wilson's brother Joseph was instrumental in developing "Lower Town," and it is for Joseph Wilson that Wilson Park in northeast St. Cloud is named.

The two great ravines at the north and south of Wilson's purchase determined the boundaries of the three settlements. "Upper Town" included the area between Fifth and Sixth Streets North up to the old Sauk Rapids Bridge. Wilson's settlement between the two ravines was known as "Middle Town." This area was plotted in 1855 and became the central business district of St. Cloud.

"Lower Town" was the settlement below the southern ravine. Brott purchased the land from a squatter and plotted the area in 1854. This was the area where the Stearns House Hotel was located, between Eighth Street South, First Avenue South, and the Mississippi River. Built in 1857, this hotel was a favorite of Southerners who came up the Mississippi to escape the oppressive heat during the summers.

A portion of only one of the ravines still remains and can be seen on Third Avenue South just on the northern edge of the St. Cloud State University campus.

In March of 1856, two years before Minnesota became a state, the three villages were combined into one town and named St. Cloud. John L. Wilson laid out the town. Wilson was of French Huguenot ancestry and chose the name for the town mainly because of his fascination with the suburb of Paris, France, called "Saint-Cloud," where the chateau that was the summer residence of Napoleon Bonaparte's wife, Josephine, is located. Undoubtedly Wilson chose the name "St. Germain," a street which used to run through the entirety of St. Cloud, after the Parisian boulevard of the same name.

St. Cloud may not have been the primary economic center of the area if disaster had not struck the area in 1886. On April 14 of that year, a tornado decimated parts of St. Cloud and Sauk Rapids (located just to the north of St. Cloud on the east side of the Mississippi). At that time, Sauk Rapids was the preeminent trading center of the area. But the tornado wreaked havoc on its commercial district. All but one public or commercial building was destroyed. The extensive damage shifted economic development towards St. Cloud, which has taken the lead ever since.

Barden Park, circa1910. Photo courtesy Stearns History Museum.

The Parks

FROM ITS BEGINNING, ST. CLOUD valued public parklands, considering them vital to its health and prosperity. In this spirit, John L. Wilson, in 1855, gave the city land for its first park. Barden Park, located between Fifth Avenue and Fourth Avenue South, was originally called Central Park because it was located in the center of the city at the time. This park was and is one block square. Since there were no streets to the south or west at the time, the park originally seemed to be more expansive because of the open wooded areas surrounding it. In 1930, the park was renamed Barden Park after Charles Barden, who, in the early 1900s, supervised St. Cloud's parks without pay. The park included a fountain and lily pond, which was later converted into a wading pool. It also housed a cannon and two large trench guns used in the Spanish-American war. A small circular flower garden was added in 1910.

Barden Park has been encroached upon by the St. Cloud State University campus (originally the campus was three blocks away). Today all that remain in Barden Park are the walkways, the green spaces and a band shell. Plans to restore the park are underway, and a copy of the original fountain has been installed.

The first park located on land purchased by the city was Empire Park, named in honor of railroad magnate James J. Hill, also known as the "Empire Builder." The Great Northern Railroad line ran just north of the park property on First Avenue North near the St. Germain bridge. Empire Park hosted brief stops by national leaders, including Presidents Theodore Roosevelt and William Howard Taft. The noise of the trains, however, contributed to the demise of Empire Park. Municipal band concerts were moved to Barden Park when a band shell was constructed in 1924. (The band shell was upgraded in 2009 by the Southside Neighborhood Historical Preservation Society.)

Empire Park ceased to exist in May of 1949 when it was paved over and became a parking lot. In September of 1968, the Housing Redevelopment Agency bought the land and built the Empire Apartments there in 1971.

A remnant of the park is the statue of Abraham Lincoln located there since 1918. In December of 2013, the Lincoln statue was moved to a site along the Mississippi riverbank close to the River's Edge Convention Center.

Between 1856 and 1930, thirteen parks came into existence in St. Cloud. Today there are ninety parks comprised of just over 1,500 acres.

Empire Park, circa 1940. Photo courtesy Stearns History Museum.

The H.J. Andersen Sawmill

THE CURRENT SITE OF MUNSINGER GARDENS was the location of the H.J. Andersen sawmill in the late nineteenth century. Hans Jacob Andersen was a Danish immigrant who arrived in the United States in 1872. In 1874, he established residence in Spring Valley, Minnesota, where he started a construction business and owned a lumber yard. He moved to La Crosse, Wisconsin, in 1887 where he purchased a wholesale lumber company. In 1889 he moved again to St. Cloud where he built the sawmill along the Mississippi. The sawmill opened in 1890. On Aug 1, 1893, a *St. Cloud Times* article noted that "the plant proper is as good as any on the Mississippi river."

Logging had its heyday in St. Cloud between 1892 and 1914. Logs floated down the Mississippi River from Little Falls. In a *St. Cloud Daily Times* article published on June 18, 1968, about the logging industry's history, it was noted that in 1879 between forty to fifty million feet of logs passed through the St. Cloud stretch of the Mississippi. The one remaining lumber yard from that era is the Mathew Hall Lumber Company located in downtown St. Cloud.

Tragedy struck the Andersen sawmill twice. It was destroyed by fire caused by lightning almost from the beginning, in 1890, and again by fire in 1897. Soon after the 1897 fire (believed to be started by arsonists), Andersen abandoned his mill and moved to Hudson, Wisconsin. He died of a heart attack in 1914. The Andersen Corporation he founded was carried on by his sons, who developed the Andersen Window and Door Company, which today is the largest wood window manufacturer in the world. Its current plant is in Bayport, Minnesota, along the St. Croix river.

The Andersen Saw Mill, circa 1891. Photo courtesy Stearns History Museum.

Riverside Park, 1920. Image courtesy Stearns History Museum.

Riverside Park

IN 1910 THE CITY OF ST. CLOUD BEGAN TO ACQUIRE the land around the abandoned Andersen Saw Mill. The land and adjacent park immediately to the south of the mill became Riverside Park, which is located south of University Avenue along Kilian Boulevard on the east side of the Mississippi River. Originally known as Eastside Park, the name was changed to Riverside Park in 1915. In 1917, 100 elm trees and 150 evergreens were planted there. In 1923, the southern portion of the park was designated as a tourist camping area, which by 1930 had six log cabins. But in 1933 the camping ground was abandoned due to lack of revenue. The "timekeeper's cabin" in Munsinger Gardens is one of those cabins, relocated to the current Gardens site in 1934.

Just south of the tourist area was Talahi Woods ("Talahi" is an Ojibwe term meaning "among the oaks"). Talahi Woods was purchased from the city of St. Cloud in 1927 for St. Cloud Teachers College by George A. Selke, president of the college. Originally, a lodge stood in the woods which became the college's most popular recreational center. Selke's intent in purchasing the property was to enhance the educational environment of the college students. There was even some speculation that someday the entire campus would be rebuilt there. This never happened. Today Talahi Woods is used for exploratory walks and instructional use for biology classes at St. Cloud State University.

When Joseph Munsinger became Superintendent of Parks in 1930, the site of the current Munsinger Gardens was part of Riverside Park and remained undeveloped. Only a few small trees and shrubs and remains of the Andersen saw mill were there.

Joseph Munsinger

Joseph Munsinger (1876-1946), the creator of today's Munsinger Gardens, moved with his family from Ontario, Canada, in 1878 when he was just two years old. His parents established a well-digging and plumbing business, and owned a saloon and a boarding house in downtown St. Cloud near Mathew Hall Lumber. According to Munsinger's son, John, the family also operated a "halfway house" on the west side of the city.

Prior to his appointment as Superintendent of Parks in St. Cloud, Munsinger worked in the plumbing and heating business and was a lieutenant in the city's fire department. By 1924, Munsinger had become actively involved in St. Cloud's park system. He first served as a member of the Park Board, then became the city weed inspector as well as the chief plumbing inspector.

In 1930 Munsinger became Park Superintendent. His charge was to improve the city's park system, which was considered run down. Munsinger was able to take advantage of the Works Public Administration (WPA) and engage laborers to help him improve the parks. The WPA was a federal program established in 1935 by President Franklin Delano Roosevelt as part of his New Deal administration. WPA was designed to put Americans back to work to help end the Great Depression. The New Deal program enlivened the development of the American public landscape. The intent of the program was to create places of enduring value for the benefit of all United States citizens.

The city of St. Cloud took advantage of the labor through not only the WPA but also the Civilian Conservation Corps (CCC) and the National Youth Administration (NYA) for various public projects throughout the city. These projects included the trimming of trees and the construction of a concrete dam and bridge at Whitney Park (located on Northway Drive) in 1938. It also included a series of granite steps in Hester Park which were completed in 1935.

When Munsinger died in 1946, the city had not only substantially improved its existing parks but also began to acquire more land for additional parks. Although he had a limited education, Joseph wrote out details of the work he had completed in each of the city parks he worked on. He recorded the building of stone walls and terraces, the planting of sod and hedges, and the addition of wading pools and tennis courts. In all, he supervised the building of city skating rinks. Munsinger oversaw the transformation of Seberger, Hester, Eastman, Empire and Wilson Parks.

Immediately following his death, an editorial in the *St. Cloud Daily Times* on April 27, 1946, praised Joseph Munsinger for his many achievements with the St. Cloud park system and described his accomplishments as a "labor of love."

Joseph Munsinger. Photo courtesy
Stearns History Museum.

The "canopied forest" provided by the tall pines shade Munsinger Gardens.

Munsinger Gardens

I N 1926 THE WEEHETONGA CAMP FIRE GIRLS had planted the Scotch and Norway pines which today provide a cathedral-like setting to the central portion of Munsinger Gardens. Larry Haws, superintendent of parks from 1948 to 1975, once commented that "Munsinger (Gardens) is probably best known for its canopied forest as well as its flowers."

The first official record of a desire to develop a portion of Riverside Park into a flower garden came when the Park Board decided in 1934 to move the "time-keeper's cabin" to its current Munsinger Gardens site. This cabin is where the WPA workers checked in and received their paychecks. A fireplace and chimney were added. It later became a public restroom area and a visitor's center.

Surrounding the cabin are four rectangular watering troughs originally used for the horses. Discontinued as watering troughs in 1916, these troughs today serve as flower planters.

Under Joseph Munsinger's supervision, the pits for the lily pond and (what is now known as) the chain-link pool were dug in 1933. Building the rock garden and ponds began in 1934 and was completed in 1935. The lily pool was built using rocks from old river beds near Popple Creek, a community located twenty-five miles east of St. Cloud. The other pool had a base of poured concrete. A fountain was placed in the center of the lily pool. A wishing well was added. Stones outlined the paths in the Garden.

Joseph Munsinger also used WPA workers to build lower granite walls along the river and throughout St. Cloud. The city now has about five thousand feet of granite walls, two thousand of those located in city parks. In addition, the workers created the original flower beds in Munsinger Gardens and began the construction of the flowering pools. Eventually these two pools, a large rock garden with steps, and several flower beds were constructed. Four thousand feet of paths were built and over one thousand yards of clay and black dirt were added to the area.

The timekeeper's cabin.

Rick Miller, the son of CCC worker Orion Miller from the Paynesville area, recollects the following:

"In the 1930's Dad served in a northern Minnesota CCC camp . . . and he deeply valued the experience. . . . Dad also valued the work of the Works Projects Administration (WPA), another FDR works program. The signature of the WPA is artistically stamped into the essence of Munsinger Gardens, with stone pools, fountains and pathways. Dad so loved the WPA's work with stone that he hand dug and lined with fieldstone a 'lily pond' on our farm house lawn, modeled after the WPA work at Munsinger."

Miller also notes:

"The trip to St. Cloud always took place between morning and evening farm chores, which meant we would have lunch in St. Cloud. . . . We all loved it though when the weather was nice, because it meant a picnic at Munsinger Gardens, which held the essence of a conifer forest intermingled with a botanical paradise."

In April 1938, the Park Board made the following decision: " . . . the part of Riverside Park north of Michigan Avenue between Riverside Drive and the Mississippi River is to be named Munsinger Gardens in honor of . . . Joseph Munsinger." A greenhouse was built in

Munsinger's natural spring-fed pool, known as the "chain-link pond."

Munsinger Gardens flowers and paths, circa 1938. Photo courtesy Stearns History Museum.

1939 to the south of Munsinger Gardens as a place to grow and cultivate the flowers for all the St. Cloud parks. In 2009, the original greenhouse was replaced by the four greenhouses in use today. These replacement greenhouses are used solely for plants and flowers in the Munsinger Clemens Gardens. New flowers for all the gardens are ordered in August for the following year. Plugs arrive throughout the winter and spring, and the flowers are grown in the Munsinger greenhouses.

Munsinger Gardens flower beds are filled annually with approximately 50,000 plants, most of which are suited to cool, moist growing conditions. This includes eighty different varieties of hosta, making it one of the largest collections of such in central Minnesota. Until recently, impatiens and begonias were used generously in areas of deep shade to lighten spaces with their bright colors. Red salvia are used for the rock wall. Other flowers vary from year to year. Meandering curved lines among the flowers and paths reflect the gentle energy and continuous movement of the nearby Mississippi River.

Stone path which mirrors the
flow of the Mississippi River

A cheerful border of early tulips.
Photo courtesy Nia Primus

Lily pond, circa 1938. Photo courtesy Stearns History Museum.

Fountain in the lily pond.

Bright red salvia cover the mound of the rock garden.

One of Joseph Munsinger's heart-shaped beds.

Munsinger's Legacy

ALTHOUGH JOSEPH MUNSINGER had no formal training as a horticulturalist, he loved flowers and possessed an innate sense of quality. He effectively used WPA workers to construct pools and the rock garden. He designed flower beds as diamond, star, and heart shapes. One of the two original heart-shaped beds remains today near the northern entrance to the garden.

Munsinger built the Williams Flower Garden which was located near Lake George. He also oversaw building bridges and retaining walls in Hester Park, located near St. Cloud Hospital. He eventually became the City Forester, overseeing the maintaining of parks and gardens and planting of trees. When he died in 1946, Munsinger was hailed by the *Times* as "the father of St. Cloud's park system and is credited with the development of St. Cloud's parks into treasured beauty spots for the city."

Another reflection on the significance of Munsinger Gardens by Rick Miller:

"Munsinger Gardens, to its visitors, has for my entire lifetime been a testament to the significance of nature's universal systems on the human psyche. The mystique of Munsinger is far more than the recording in one's own mind of the visual images and aromas of the park. Munsinger is a place rich in sensory enlightenment, a place that offers therapeutic perspective and a place that can connect us to the spiritual in the word's deepest sense of meaning. . . . A consciousness desperately needed to lift our society out of its dependence on material consumption and into the quest to discover the path to an appreciation for, and commitment to, the community of human relationship."

The Granite City

MUNSINGER BUILT GRANITE WALLS BECAUSE GRANITE had become one of the primary industries in the area. St. Cloud had become known as the "busy, gritty granite city." Local rock and granite have served to embrace the regional spirit of Munsinger Gardens. All the granite used in the construction of Munsinger Gardens comes from within a ten-mile radius of the site. The granite walls in Munsinger Gardens can be seen as one approaches Riverside Drive from several of the side streets leading towards the Gardens, revealing the importance of granite to Munsinger and the early residents of St. Cloud.

A 1921 booklet entitled *St. Cloud Minnesota. The Granite City of the World Bids You Welcome* describes St. Cloud granite as "a pure syenite consisting of hornblende, feldspar and quartz, three of the most durable materials known to science." The granite industry developed rapidly in the 1880s through the efforts of Scottish, Swedish and Polish immigrants. The first granite quarry was established in 1863 by Breen and Young Granite Company, and the St. Cloud Reformatory near Highway 10 in southeast St. Cloud was built in 1889 on the site of this quarry. The granite wall that surrounds the Reformatory, completed in 1939, is purported to be second in length only to the Great Wall of China, and the longest uninterrupted wall in the world (the Great Wall is interrupted by gates).

By 1914 there were four major St. Cloud granite companies, the largest being the St. Cloud Iron Works. By 1920 there were fifty quarry and cutting firms. St. Cloud's granite industry initially provided the granite paving blocks forming the bed for the street railways in Minneapolis and St. Paul. St. Cloud paving blocks were shipped as far away as St. Louis. As St. Cloud gained in stature, granite was used in the construction of state and federal buildings throughout the area.

Besides its use in roads and buildings, another mainstay of the granite industry was the creation of cemetery headstones and markers. This sustained the industry when other aspects of the granite business began to slack off during the Great Depression. But by 1960, cemeteries began using small flat markers at gravesites, and the market for granite headstones significantly dwindled.

Left: Granite staircase found in Hester Park.

Below: A wall built of local granite blocks.

Developments Since Joseph Munsinger

I N 1946 MUNSINGER GARDENS BECAME the responsibility of Joseph Krakowski, a retired Polish farmer. Al Bauer took over in 1958, and John E. Dubbin became the Gardens foreman in 1972. The position of Superintendent of Parks was held by Phil Nierengarten from 1948 to 1975. Larry Haws assumed this position from 1975 to 2002. Roger Kapsch was Parks Director for one year and Prentice Foster was appointed to this position from 2003 until 2007. After Foster's tenure, Scott Zlotnik took over and assumed the title of Park and Recreation Director in 2010.

In 1956 a chain-link fence was added to the natural spring-fed pool to keep neighborhood kids out, and also because stray boulders were being tossed in there.

In 1968 a long-range plan was adopted by the city of St. Cloud to preserve and improve the beauty of the Mississippi River. Soon after, large boulders along the riverbank were added to replace an original granite wall built by the WPA, which had deteriorated.

Since the late 1960s, an enduring feature of Munsinger Gardens has been the cages containing assorted birds, including the famed Munsinger peacocks which delight visitors who stroll towards the Visitors Center and picnic area located just to the south of the Gardens.

In the fall of 1989 a gazebo was built for the garden by students from the St. Cloud Technical College. Originally a site to celebrate the Tri-College picnic held each Fall in the 1980s and '90s, this gazebo is now used for a variety of purposes, such as for Theater in the Park productions, family gatherings, and official ceremonies.

Granite benches and naturalistic wooden benches were given as memorials starting in 1999. This practice has been discontinued as it became burdensome for the Park Department to maintain.

Munsinger Gardens has retained its role as the city's public flower garden largely due to the support of the St. Cloud community and the financial creativity of the

Park Department. Other sources of financial support include the St. Cloud Granite Rotary Club, which helped provide the Munsinger Gardens sign, the renovation of the timekeeper's cabin, and the building of the Special Events area at the northern end of the Gardens.

Left: Large granite boulders replace a WPA era wall.

Below: The current Gardens sign, donated by the St. Cloud Granite Rotary club.

The gazebo, built in 1989, by students from St. Cloud Techical College.

Walking paths and ornamental lighting along the Mississippi River in Munsinger Gardens

David Morreim

In 1983, David Morreim, a native of St. Cloud, became the city's nursery supervisor. He graduated from St. John's University, where he worked for five years as greenhouse assistant to Father Gunther Rolfson, a botany professor. With Father Gunther, Morreim began his garden tours of Europe. He traveled there nine times, studying various gardens and gathering ideas for the development of St. Cloud's gardens. After graduation, he furthered his horticultural education with classes at the University of Minnesota.

Under Morreim's leadership, many new developments and improvements were instituted. Reminiscent of Munsinger's use of the WPA, Morreim used labor provided by the Housing and Redevelopment Agency (HRA) to develop the site. Paths were widened and new flower beds were installed. Four crescent beds were added along Riverside Drive, and the half-moon bed around the Munsinger Gardens sign was enlarged to a full circle in 1997. Several improvements were made along the Mississippi riverbank, including the installation of ornamental lighting, granite benches, and swinging wooden benches overlooking the Mississippi.

In 1993, a cement retaining wall was added to the lily pond, and window box-style planters were added to emphasize the outline of the pond. Helping to obscure its edge and to blend the pool with its naturalistic surroundings, the plants in these beds have become an integral part of the lily pond's design. Flower beds were also added to the chain-link pool.

Morreim began the expansion of the gardens with the "up the hill" Formal Garden on Kilian Boulevard. This expansion caught the eye of William Clemens, leading to the creation of the entire Clemens Gardens. Clemens, who lived just across the street, began to engage Morreim in discussions about this new garden and the possibility for developing additional gardens. Morreim dreamed them all up, submitted a master plan, and Clemens offered financial assistance. David Morreim brought them into existence with the help of his coworkers.

Morreim resigned his position with the city in 2000 and now runs Pattison Farms in northwest St. Cloud. He also devotes his time and energies to harvesting a large vegetable garden which helps stock area food shelves, and he conducts gardening workshops in St. Cloud area schools.

Below: David Morreim.

Below: One of the swinging benches installed during David Morreim's tenure.

Julie Dierkhising

Julie Dierkhising became part of the Munsinger work crew in 1986. In 1990 she was hired to be David Morreim's assistant because of her extensive knowledge of plants. They had developed a good working relationship, and she graduated from St. Cloud State University with a major in Biology. In 2000 she succeeded Morreim as Gardens Supervisor. During her tenure, Dierkhising's plans for the beds typically incorporated a traditional mix of annuals and perennials as Joseph Munsinger's had, and she gradually replaced older inferior perennials with more disease-resistant varieties.

Julie Dierkhising. Photo courtesy Munsinger Clemens Botanical Society.

Nia Primus has added succulents in the garden.

Nia Primus

Nia Primus became the Gardens Supervisor in December of 2010.

As Gardens Supervisor, Nia Primus has not changed the basic format of the Gardens, but she continually researches techniques of modern gardening and keeps abreast of new types of plants. She also believes in cooperation, as successful design and maintenance of the Gardens need to be a team effort. Primus designs and takes care of the Rest Area Garden but allows the staff to work with her and come up with designs for the other areas of the park. When Primus orders flowers from the catalog, she consults with her gardeners. Under her supervision, no two years of plantings are exactly the same. Through her continual research and study of the latest trends in plants and flowers, she orders something new each year. One area that reflects her unique creativity is her work with succulents and cacti, which she has been introducing to the gardens in recent years.

In 2012 and 2013 *impatiens walleriana* found in the Munsinger Gardens were killed by downy mildew (*plasmopara obducens*) which plagued many other areas of the U.S. Beginning in 2013, Primus and the Gardens staff have planted New Guinea impatiens, wax begonias, tuberous begonia, and torenia in the areas where *impatiens walleriana* used to grow.

In addition, Nia Primus has visions for revamping the Special Events Area, hoping possibly to have it rebuilt. She also would like to upgrade the lily pond which she has ascertained needs improvement.

Clemens Gardens

THE DEVELOPMENT OF THE CLEMENS GARDENS began in the mid-1980s. Initially an extension of Munsinger Gardens, the Clemens Gardens has become a distinctive entity of its own. Most of the land (excluding the lot where the Rose Garden now exists) was donated to the city by Earl D. and Fritz Cross between 1910 and 1920. The area was originally a gravel pit.

Joseph Munsinger expressed an interest in improving the site in 1932. In 1939 the area was still undeveloped. Finally in 1941, a recommendation was made to smooth out the land and to have city workers plant trees and shrubs. The site was developed into a neighborhood park, featuring an open green space and a hockey and skating rink for winter recreation.

In 1985 David Morreim and the park staff decided to begin developing a new garden at the top of the hill on Kilian Boulevard. According to Morreim, who was largely responsible for its inception and design, this garden was established "with a few sod cutters, some wheelbarrows, one pick-up truck and lots of strength and determination." Using hand shovels, workers removed and replaced eighteen inches of soil with a custom made blend of peat, black dirt, and sand. The basic structure of the garden was a circle set within a larger square, and the majority of the original flowers used were annuals, such as petunias, geraniums, marigolds, begonias and delphiniums.

Clemens Gardens now consists of six formal gardens located in the northern portion of Riverside Park on the upper terrace of the Mississippi River basin. The boundaries for these Gardens are Kilian Boulevard, University Avenue, and Thirteenth Street Southeast. Two private residences are also located on the site.

In the center of the Clemens Gardens is the Formal Garden, which initiated the development of what became a series of the six distinctive gardens, which will be described in more detail in the following pages. These gardens continually display a wide variety of plants that can be grown in full-sun conditions in central

Above: Top of the Clemens Garden
staircase, facing north.

Left: An urn filled with
bright coleus.

Minnesota. They have been patterned on elements of English and other European gardens, but have been adapted to St. Cloud's particular climate.

The layers of color and textures in all of the Clemens Gardens flower beds provide a proverbial feast for the eye with their explosions of color set off by various shades and hues of green.

The interesting contours formed by the creative trimming of various small trees, hedges and bushes cause the visitor to feel an inspiring symmetry in the design of these gardens. The six gardens were designed as outdoor garden rooms, each one leading into the other.

Overlooking the Clemens Gardens.

Statue in the Rose Garden of William and Virginia Clemens.

The Clemens Legacy

In THE MID-1980s, William and Virginia Clemens gave over $5.6 million dollars to the city of St. Cloud for the creation of the six Clemens Gardens. An additional endowment of $2 million was established in 1994 and is managed by the Central Minnesota Community Foundation to be used for the upkeep and maintenance of the Gardens.

The Clemens home is located across the street on Kilian Boulevard. William Clemens, born in 1920, originally came from Fargo, North Dakota. He attended St. John's University in Collegeville and met his future wife, Virginia Weitzel, who was working at Fandel's Department Store (at the current Herberger's site) in downtown St. Cloud. They were married in 1943 in Quantico, Virginia, while he was serving in the U.S. Navy and Virginia was working for the FBI.

In 1984 the Clemenses purchased the land that became the Rose Garden and donated it to the city. In 1990, William commissioned the creation of the Rose Garden as a way to improve his wife's view from their home. Virginia Clemens had multiple sclerosis, which necessitated spending much of her later years at home.

David Morreim had dreamed of developing a rose garden, and since Virginia's middle name was Rose, the current site seemed to be the perfect spot. The generous gift and subsequent endowment from William and Virginia Clemens ensured that there would be permanent funding to create and maintain all six of the Clemens Gardens.

Throughout the years, both William and Virginia Clemens have contributed ideas and perspectives to the development of the six Clemens Gardens. When David Morreim was conceptualizing the White Garden, Virginia insisted he travel to Sissinghurst Castle in Kent, England, to view the gardens there, and the Clemenses provided funds for him to do so. She was also instrumental in choosing the fountains, fences, urns, and iron benches that grace each of the Clemens Gardens. Prior to Virginia's death in 1998, William would bring her

Bill and Virginia Clemens. Photo courtesy Clemens family.

over to the Gardens daily during the regular season to inspect them. To this day, William can be seen regularly crossing the street to enjoy the Gardens.

The bronze statue of William and Virginia was created by artists Tina Sten Haugen and Donald Haugen of Marietta, Georgia. One of William and Virginia's daughters, Mary Sue Potter, and her husband Durand Potter (who are currently the trustees of all of the Clemens endowment funds) oversaw its creation. The Clemens children have donated the gazebo and pillars which house the statue in the Rest Area Garden near the Rose Garden, and also a memorial "Rose piece" pillar sculpture.

William and Virginia, who grew up during the Great Depression, considered their philanthropic endeavors to be a necessary part of life, as gratitude for the success bestowed upon them. Their generosity in establishing the Clemens Gardens has given St. Cloud a permanent treasure to be enjoyed for years to come.

The Virginia Clemens Rose Garden

THE ROSE GARDEN, CONSTRUCTED AS A RAISED RECTANGLE with a border of red brick, is attractively laid out in a concentric circular pattern with a fountain in the middle, and includes 1,800 roses. These roses come from all over the world, with only one rose being unique to St. Cloud: the Virginia Clemens rose. The design of this garden causes it to stand out from other such gardens as an exceptional display area for all the variety of roses featured there.

At the rear of these gardens is the Rose piece pillar sculpture with its inscription given by the Clemens children to honor their mother.

Since its inception, the Rose Garden has had a rose expert (known as a Rosarian) in charge of overseeing, maintaining and labeling the roses. The first Rosarian, Nancy Caspers, had a horticultural degree from Brainerd Technical College and began working at the Clemens Gardens in 1990. Steve Gessell from the Becker Power Plant took over from 1992 to 2000. After four years of temporary staffing, Deb Keiser became the Rosarian in 2004.

Under the guidance of Deb Keiser, the Rose Garden became an All-America Rose Selections (AARS) test garden. AARS is a nonprofit association dedicated to the introduction and promotion of exceptional roses. Gardens selected for this designation are chosen based on the excellence of roses during a two-year trial program. Similar AARS gardens are located in nine different states, most notably the Portland, Oregon Rose Garden and the Chicago Botanical Gardens. To the south of the formal Rose Garden are now two ancillary test rose gardens, originally chosen for the AARS roses. Although the Clemens Rose Garden is no longer an AARS designated garden, different flower companies have continued to contract with it to test grow a variety of roses to decide how marketable these roses might become. The normal testing period is two years. After that, flower companies determine whether or not to pursue future development and sale of a particular species.

A variety of roses found in the Virgina Clemens Rose Garden.

Rest Area Garden

THE REST AREA GARDEN LOCATED IN FRONT OF THE gift shop and public restrooms officially opened in the spring of 1993. It features a mix of pastel flowers, including trellises covered with flowering clematis and rose vines. David Morreim chose plants of pink, white and lavender, which were Virginia Clemens' favorite colors and Nia Primus continues the tradition of using pastel colors in this garden, but is now mixing in flowers with bolder colors as well. She also has used a variety of ornamental grasses of different heights to add varied interest.

The Rest Area Garden is unique in that it contains one of the tallest outdoor fountains in Minnesota, the Renaissance Fountain with Cranes. Visitors are encouraged to throw in a coin on the three tiers of the fountain or relax on one of the botanical settees.

This garden is located in front of the gift shop and the public restrooms. Behind the gift shop there is a deck where visitors can sit and gaze upon the winding walkways under the pine trees, lined with hostas, that lead down the hill to Munsinger Gardens.

The pathway and garden leading to the gift shop.

Top: Ornamental grasses enhance the gardens.

Right: The contrast of smooth turf and clipped hedges add to the textures of the gardens.

The Formal Garden

THIS IS THE GARDEN THAT STARTED IT ALL, initially installed in 1986 as an extension of Munsinger Gardens in which to grow sun-loving flowers. This garden now contains a mixture of both annuals and perennials, with different varieties of annuals planted from year to year. In contrast to the Rest Area Garden, this garden features bright colored flowers. It is considered "formal" because of the squared off paths, and the challenge of maintaining this garden is ensuring that the paths are uniform on all sides.

The White Garden

THE WHITE GARDEN HAS BEEN PATTERNED after the famous white garden at Sissinghurst Castle. The flowers used here are not all the same as in England due to climatic differences, but two-thirds of the Sissinghurst varieties are found here. To create the White Garden, David Morreim traveled to England to view the Sissinghurst Castle and to plot out the design of those gardens. Morreim says that since Sissinghurst has a more temperate climate than Minnesota, the choice of flowers in the White Garden has evolved through trial-and-error. Substitutes which grew better here included white tulips, daffodils, hyacinth, peonies and lilies.

In relation to size, the White Garden has acquired more decorative accents than any of the other Clemens Gardens. Patterned after the Sissinghurst gardens, cast iron urns are used to mark both entrances to this garden, and four large planters were placed at its outer corners to serve as anchors. The junipers that used to surround the garden had to be taken out because of moisture problems.

Opposite above: Cast iron, brick, and the lush green bring out the bright white of the White Garden flowers.

Opposite below: Feathery astilbe contrasts with white peonies and sweet alyssum in the White Garden.

The Perennial Garden

COLD-HARDY PERENNIALS ARE FEATURED in this garden that can survive the tough Minnesota winters. Plants were carefully chosen by Morreim, and many of the original plants remain from this garden's inception in 1995. The Perennial Garden is patterned after the English cottage garden style, which favors asymmetry to structure, with more informal planting. This style became popular in the latter half of the nineteenth century and uses selected perennials to provide a lavish display of color.

A midsummer explosion of color in the Perennial Garden

The Treillage Garden

DAVID MORREIM GOT HIS IDEAS AND CHOSE elements from existing English gardens during his numerous trips to Europe to create the four monochromatic gardens surrounding the vine-covered treillage (trellis). Designed by Wayne Fuller of Alabama, the trellis patterned after a similar treillage at Easton Lodge in England. The arbor is over 100 feet long and features a 24-foot high central dome, which has been fortified to support the vine cover and the winter snow which adds weight to it. The arbor had to be constructed at Robinson Iron and shipped to St. Cloud. The garden as a whole provides one of the biggest challenges to create and maintain, due in part to the treillage itself, and because of the difficulty in finding monochromatic plants for each of the gardens.

Choosing plants for the Blue Garden was and is the biggest challenge since not many blue plants can give season-long blue color in Minnesota. Originally delphiniums, blue salvia and bachelor buttons were selected. Some perennials have been added that start out the season with a more purplish huc, but become more bluish in color as the season progresses.

The easiest garden to create and maintain in Minnesota summers was the Yellow Garden with its abundance of daffodils in the spring, lilies and marigolds in the summer, and 'mums in the fall.

The Purple and Red Gardens were based on similar designs found in England. Japanese maple and sand cherries were added to the Red Garden in 1994, to provide foliage that would be exciting and dramatic and last most of the growing season. However, the Japanese maples had to be removed due to winter kill. A Shenandoah grass has recently been added, which turns red in the Fall.

The Yellow Garden features a circle of turf in the center.

Red Treilliage Garden.

The Bue Garden (above) and the Purple Garden (below).

The rose piece pillar in the Rose Garden. Inscription: "A solitary woman defined by her spirit touching countless lives. In loving memory of our mother Virginia Rose Clemens."

Robinson Iron Works

THE BRONZE FOUNTAINS FOUND IN EACH of the six gardens and the fences surrounding the Gardens were made by Robinson Iron of Alexander City, Alabama. Robinson Iron, which has provided statuary and fountains for gardens, historical and cultural sites across the nation and the world, came to David Morreim's attention when he spotted an ad in a *Garden Design* magazine and contacted the company for more information. The fences around the Rose Garden were built first to deter people from stealing and trampling on the roses. Robinson Iron then sent John Allen to look over the Gardens and create a master plan for the fountains, which they subsequently named.

The Windsor Court Fountain.

The Renaissance Fountain.

Fountains and Urns

ALL OF THE FOUNTAINS WERE DONATED BY Virginia Clemens, who up until her death consulted with Morreim and her family on design ideas. Collaboratively they chose the designs for the fountains, metal benches, urns, planters, gate fencing, and signage which grace the entirety of the Clemens Gardens. The final decision was almost always made by Virginia herself. Two of the large urns in the Clemens Gardens have been donated by Robinson Iron.

The most spectacular fountain is the twenty-four-foot high **Renaissance Fountain with Cranes** located in the Rest Area Garden. Weighing 9,000 pounds, and measuring over twelve feet in diameter, this multi-tiered fountain features bathing boys on the lower level, cranes spouting water from a perch above them, and the figure of Hebe, cupbearer to the Greek gods, on the top tier. Decorative shells and scrolls on each tier complete the fountain. Though St. Cloud is known as the Granite City, the granite on the fountain came from Brazil, because its black color matches the patina of the cast iron.

The **Janney Crane Fountain** in the center of the Rose Garden creates a light mist to enhance the roses surrounding it. This fountain is a replica of a pre-Civil War fountain in Columbus, Georgia. A Janney fountain is a three-tiered fountain which demonstrates the precise relationship between technical and artistic vision. This solid cast iron piece of cranes and foliage is detailed by framed scrolled borders.

In the center of the Formal Garden is the **Windsor Court Fountain**, a low two-tiered fountain featuring bathing swans made of bronze. Patterned after a similar fountain in Charleston, South Carolina, these finely crafted swans maintain a delicate presence while supporting the two tiers of this stylish fountain.

The **Three Graces Fountain** standing in the middle of the Treillage Garden depicts Hebe standing atop the fountain. A light trickle of water overflows her cup. Under her stand the three graces: joy, bloom, and brilliance, representing the talents of music and the arts. This fountain was the first fountain accentuated with bronze sculptures.

Above: Janney Crane Fountain.

Opposite: Three Graces Fountain.

Below: Placing the second tier of the Renaissance Fountain. Photo courtesy *St. Cloud Times*.

Fences, Gates &
Benches

LIKE THE FOUNTAINS, THE FENCES AND GATES surrounding several of the Clemens Gardens were also built by Robinson Iron. Although the gates are not locked during the Gardens' season, they do serve as a deterrent from abusing the numerous flowers and plants in the Clemens Gardens. They also serve as an attractive frame, adding to the aura of the Gardens.

Benches with hoofed feet are found at each end of the Rose Garden, and are patterned after settees in the Shaw Botanical Garden in St. Louis, Missouri.

An elaborate iron bench made by Robinson Iron.

An iron gate (above) and bench (right) made by Robinson Iron.

Music in the Gardens in Munsinger Gardens.

Community Activities

BOTH MUNSINGER AND CLEMENS GARDENS have become popular venues for weddings and other special events at not only the Special Events area, but throughout the gardens.

Use of the gardens for weddings and family photos can be arranged with St. Cloud's Park and Recreation office.

In 1999 retired St. Cloud State University Music Professor Kenton Frohrip conceived a series of concerts to be held in Munsinger Gardens. Attracting hundreds of Saint Cloud residents, the free Music in the Gardens concerts are presented by Munsinger Clemens Botanical Society (MCBS) and have become a popular staple of the community.

People bring their lawn chairs to sit and listen to quality music performances by such groups as the George Maurer Jazz Ensemble, the Lake Wobegon Brass Ensemble, Ring of Kerry and other groups.

Music in the Gardens has spawned a myriad of summertime artistic activities which are also sponsored by the MCBS, such as Theater in the Gardens, held at the gazebo and co-sponsored by the Great River Educational Arts Theatre (GREAT), an annual art fair, and an annual photography contest for aspiring camera bugs.

The Special Events Area

2011 Photo contest winner of the Munsing Clemens Botanical Society. Photo courtes Suzanna Johnson.

2013 Photo contest winner of the Munsinger Clemens Botanical Society. Photo courtesy Don Kempf.

Community Support

OVER THE YEARS, MEMBERS OF THE local community have contributed time and money to the development of Munsinger and Clemens Gardens. Volunteer workers mingle with paid staff to help with the upkeep of the gardens. In 1995 Larry Haws approached local radio station WJON owner Andy Hilger to launch a fund drive to help upgrade the Munsinger Clemens Gardens. Within a few short weeks $80,000 was raised from individuals.

The Central Minnesota Builders Association assisted in building the gift shop and public restrooms. The St. Cloud Granite Rotary Club has given over $190,000. In addition to the Munsinger Gardens sign on Riverside Drive, the Granite Rotary Club also helped build the Activities Center and restore the timekeeper's cabin.

In 1989 the St. Cloud Technical College built and installed the current gazebo close to the river, which houses many special events at Munsinger Gardens.

In 1999 **the Munsinger Clemens Botanical Society** (MCBS) began under the leadership of Terry Engels and Karen Frohrip. Members of this Society continue to volunteer at many of these events and to provide money for equipment items needed to maintain the gardens.

In 2005 the **Friends of the Gardens** organization was formed by bringing together three entities: the Clemens family, St. Cloud Granite Rotary, and Munsinger Clemens Botanical Society, along with community and neighborhood representatives. This group has raised money for augmenting the upkeep and maintenance of the gardens. To date they have contributed over $390,000 for such purposes.

Bela Petheo paintings

Artistic Representations of Munsinger Gardens

THE BEAUTY OF THE MUNSINGER CLEMENS GARDENS inspires many artists. Most notable is Bela Petheo, an artist who is now retired from St. John's University. Petheo completed several commissions from the Botanical Society and the Clemens family. Two of his works now hang in the Mayor's office in downtown St. Cloud, and one depicting a Music in the Gardens concert hangs in the office of the Central Minnesota Community Foundation.

Also notable is a sizable triptych of Munsinger Gardens which hung in the lobby of the Le Saint Germain hotel in downtown St. Cloud. The triptych was created by Michael Popilek, a freelance artist who resides in Chicago.

Interior designer R.C. McCoy, who lives on Kilian Boulevard across from the Gardens, was instrumental in designing the Clemens Gardens gift shop and public restrooms. He is also a painter, and his painting of the gazebo and its Mississippi River setting is on display at the St. Cloud Foot and Ankle Clinic on Northway Drive.

Gerald Korte, an art professor at St. Cloud State University, was commissioned in 1996 to do a special painting for his longtime colleague and friend Jack Kelly and his wife Doris. The painting is of Munsinger Gardens, and hangs in the Kelly home on Riverside Drive.

Gerald Korte painting

Right: Center panel of tryptich by Mike Pokilek.

Below: R.C. McCoy painting.

Opposite: Red Trelliage Garden flowers.

Legacy

In its early years, Munsinger Gardens began as a flower park maintained by volunteers. With the hiring of Joseph Munsinger as St. Cloud's first park supervisor, these gardens were transformed into an area of unbelievable beauty. Thanks to the generous philanthropy of Bill and Virginia Clemens and the creativity of park supervisor David Morreim, Clemens Gardens began in the late 1980s and developed into a series of elegant gardens which enthrall the thousands of visitors who come to enjoy them each year.

The Munsinger Clemens Gardens bring in visitors from all over the world. Truly these Gardens, with their spectacular natural setting and perpetual beauty, will continue to captivate the hearts and minds of all who come to view them. Whether coming to the Gardens for a wedding, or to enjoy an arts event, or just to take a leisurely stroll and admire their beauty, the experience will long be remembered and serve to solidify the reputation of these Gardens as "the Jewel of St. Cloud."

Bibliography

BOOKS

Burke, S.l. and Wright, C.S. *St. Cloud, Minnesota, The Granite City Bids You Welcome.* Greater St. Cloud Committee of the Chamber of Commerce and Federal Writers Project, Works Progress Administration. St. Cloud, MN: 1936.

Dominik, John J. *St. Cloud, The Triplet City.* Windsor Publications, Inc. Woodland Hills, CA: 1983.

Dominik, John J. and Massmann, John C. *St. Cloud, The Triplet City*, 2nd edition. American Historical Press Sun Valley, CA: 2002.

Dominik, John J. *Three Towns into One City: St. Cloud, Minnesota.* The St. Cloud Area Bicentennial Commission. July 27, 1978.

Gove, Gertrude B. *A History of St. Cloud, Minnesota, 1853-1970.* Delta Kappa Gamma. Graphics Art of Technical High School. St. Cloud, MN: 1970.

Gove, Gertrude. *St. Cloud Centennial Souvenier Album (1856-1956).* St. Cloud Centennial Committee. St.. Cloud, MN: 1956.

Johnson, Ann Marie. *St. Cloud's Clemens and Munsinger Gardens: A Public Legacy* A Thesis for the degree Master of Arts. St. Cloud State University. St. Cloud, MN: August, 1998.

League of Minnesota Municipalities Convention. *Souvenier of the City of St. Cloud.* The League of Minnesota Municipalities. October 17-18, 1917.

Price, Susan D. *Minnesota Gardens: An Illustrated History.* Afton Historical Society Press. Afton, MN: 1995.

Seberger, P.J. *St. Cloud, Its Historical Background and As It Is Today.* St. Cloud Daily Times and Northstar Printing Co. St. Cloud, MN: 1931.

Zosel, Harold. *St. Cloud* (Postcard Historical Series). Arcadia Publishing. Charleston, SC: 2010.

ARTICLES

"Andersen Saw Mill destroyed by fire," *St. Cloud Daily Times*, August 9, 1897.

"Behold the Munsinger charm," *St. Cloud Times,* August 13, 2004: p. 1C.

"Fountains soon to enhance Clemens," *St. Cloud Times*, April 16, 1992: p. 3A.

"The Gardens," *St. Cloud Times*, January 25, 1995: p. 12.

"H.J. Andersen, Danish immigrant, visited St. Cloud in 1889," *St. Cloud Daily Times*, August 1, 1893.

"New Fountain Graces Clemens Gardens," *St. Cloud Times*, April 10, 1998: p. 3A.

"Munsinger and Clemens Gardens," *Crossings,* Stearns County Historical Society, September, 1998.

"Rock-solid good time in Granite City," Minneapolis *Star-Tribune*, September 16, 2012, Travel section: p. 1.

"St. Cloud Mourns Death of Father of Our Park System," *St. Cloud Daily Times*, April 27, 1946: p. 4.

"State's biggest fountain coming," *St. Cloud Times*, July 22, 1998: p. 1A.

Berquist, Kris, "The Rose," *St. Cloud Times*, December 5, 1993: p. 1B.

Blomker, Bryan. "Munsinger Park prepared for a new season," *Impressions*. B and K Publications [St. Cloud, MN], May, 1981: pp. 34ff.

Bowen, Amy. "Behind the Gardens," *St. Cloud Times*, July 24, 1991: p. 1B.

Dubois, John. "Benevolence Blooms at the Virginia Clemens Rose Garden," St. Cloud Department of Parks and Recreation, 1992.

Dubois, John. "Munsinger Gardens' fund grows greener with Sale," *St. Cloud Times*, September 5, 1991: p. 1B.

Hargrave, Jennifer. "Munsinger Gardens," St. Cloud Park Office: 1996.

Kuluza, Rene. "Clemens family establishes fund for community improvements," *St. Cloud Times*, January 4, 1995.

Lehrke, Mrs. George W. "Park History," *St. Cloud Daily Times*, September 30, 1945: p. 9.

McClintick, Lisa. "Virginia Clemens Dies at 77," *St. Cloud Times*, August 31, 1998: p. 1.

Olsen, Roberta. "Munsinger, Clemens Gardens give rest to the soul," *Melrose Beacon*, July 18, 2009: p. 1B.

Riebe, Tammy Jo. "Clemens stays quiet over plans for gardens," *St. Cloud Times*, August 31, 1998: p. 3A.

Schumacher, Lawrence. "Statue to Honor Couple," *St. Cloud Times*, July 21, 2009.

Vossler, Bill. "The Prized Gardens of St. Cloud." *FMC Magazine*. Family Motor Coach Association, July 2008,

Voth, Irene. "Virginia Clemens remembered for her cheerfulness, benevolence," [ed. Bishop John Kinney], *St. Cloud Visitor*, Pastoral Center-Diocese of St. Cloud, September 3, 1998.

VIDEOS

Clemens Gardens. Bankers Systems. 1996.

Jewel of St. Cloud: Munsinger and Glemens Gardens. Produced by Jason VanderEyk and Candace Leyk. St. Cloud Media Division. 2006

POWERPOINT

Munsinger/Clemens Powerpoint. Munsinger Clemens Botanical Society. St. Cloud, MN. 2004.

WEBSITES

"Clemens Gardens Named." Produced by Jim Maurice. http://wjon.com/clemens-gardens-named-on-this-date-in-central-minnesota-history/. WJON Radio. July 20, 2011.

"Clemens Gardens." http://www.ci.stcloud.mn.us/index.aspx?NID=192. City of St. Cloud. 2013.

"Munsinger /Clemens Gardens." http://www.ci.stcloud.mn.us/index.aspx?NID=161. City of St. Cloud. 2013.

"Munsinger Clemens Gardens." http://www.youtube.com/watch?v=5YNeCAuFTDM. 2013

"Renaissance with Cranes (Clemens Gardens)." http://www.robinsoniron.com/fountains_lg/clemens_garden.html. 2013.

http://www.munsingerclemens.com/ MunsingerClemens Botanical Society. 2013.

http://www.tripadvisor.com/Attraction_Review-g43493-d273815-Reviews-Munsinger_Gardens-Saint_Cloud_Minnesota.html. 2013.

http://en.wikipedia.org/wiki/Munsinger_Gardens_and_Clemens_Gardens. 2013.

http://aroundthecloud.org/venue/detail/67/Munsinger_Clemens_Gardens. 2013.

http://www.ask.com/wiki/Munsinger_Gardens_and_Clemens_Gardens. February, 2013.

About the Author

Stephen Fuller is a Professor Emeritus of Music at St. Cloud State University, having served on the music faculty there from 1975-2010. For nineteen years he was Director of Choral Activities, and for eleven years he was Graduate Coordinator for the Music Department graduate programs. Prior to teaching at SCSU, Fuller taught at the University of Hawaii-Hilo from 1968-1973. He served in the US Army in Vietnam. He has been organist/choirmaster at several Lutheran churches in Minnesota and in California. From 1983-85 Fuller was a visiting professor of choral music at Luther College in Decorah, Iowa. In 2004 he was Academic Director for the SCSU British Studies program at the Alnwick Castle in England. Fuller has also published articles on Japanese music.

In addition to his musical accomplishments, Fuller is an avid outdoor enthusiast with a genuine appreciation of nature. Fuller loves gardening, hiking, biking, bird watching and exploring surrounding wildlife. He also loves to travel and has carried out these activities on several continents. Since retirement he is active as a piano recitalist, as a singer in the Great River Chorale and as a member of St. Cloud Kiwanis. He has also expanded his interest in photography.